Poverty Prepping

How to stock up for tomorrow
When you can't afford to eat today!

By Susan Gregersen

Copyright April 2012

Dedicated to everyone who ever wondered where their next meal was coming from, and to my kindred spirits who have also dug through couch cushions and their car looking for change!

Thank you, to my wonderful husband, Steven, for his help and encouragement in writing this!

Table of Contents

Introduction

I've heard a lot of people say they can't store extra food because they don't have the money. Many people who are interested in "prepping", or preparedness, have spent time on Internet forums devoted to the subject, or read books and newspaper articles about it. They quickly become overwhelmed by the discussions about how much to store, what types of food to store, and how to store it.

It seems like a daunting task to accomplish, especially if you have little or no money to work with. You may even give up before you start

You don't need to buy expensive Freeze-dried long-term food-storage items, or nitro-packed wheat, or any of the other luxury food storage items. They're nice to have if you have the money to buy them, but a lot of us don't.

Being among the "financially challenged" segment of society I consider it an accomplishment whenever I can afford one extra of anything. That might be a can of salt, a bag of noodles, or even a 50-lb. bag of rice!

The important thing is that if something happens, such as a power outage, huge snowstorm, or possibly an economic, political, or war type disaster, I have something in the house to keep us fed, at least for a while.

People worry about how much to store. At our end of the money spectrum, it's more of a question of having ANYTHING to store, so my philosophy is you start with one thing. I've heard a story about how to eat an elephant. You do it "One bite at a time". That's what we're going to do with prepping.

We're going to learn how to take that first bite, and how to keep taking bites. I can't tell you when you'll be done eating the elephant. Maybe never. Maybe you'll keep adding to your stores, then need to use them, then add more again. Maybe you'll have to live on them for years. Maybe nothing will ever happen, and you'll have to shove some of it off on your family, friends, or neighbors before it gets too old to eat.

But at least you'll have it if you need it. And with my poverty prepping plan, you won't even feel the pinch as you build up your reserves.

I believe you can be a prepper for $20 or less per month.

Chapter 1

Why Store Food Anyway?

We live in a land of plenty here in the United States. There are grocery stores in every town, convenience stores scattered everywhere. Even hardware stores, video game shops, and just about every place we go have snacks and drinks for sale.

Most of us have income in the form of paychecks from our jobs, and others have checks from retirement funds of one kind or another.

We have a safety net for those in need, in the form of other types of checks and food assistance programs. The most commonly known one is food stamps. In addition to that program there are food banks run by various organizations in many towns and cities, as well as soup kitchens and other meal programs.

FEMA, the Red Cross, and others have plans and supplies to help when natural disasters occur. I know this hasn't functioned as well as hoped, but they are always working to improve their preparedness plans.

So, again… why store food? I can think of a lot of reasons. Fresh in our minds is Hurricane Katrina. Resources were stretched beyond thin. There wasn't enough to go around, and the disaster was too wide-spread to reach everyone in a timely manner.

New England has been hammered with some pretty big snowstorms the last couple of winters. Electricity was off for days in some areas, and driving anywhere wasn't safe while trees, limbs, and lines were down.

Hurricane Sandy devastated New York City and surrounding areas in October 2012, leaving millions without electricity, food, or gasoline.

Tornadoes have been known to tear up wide swaths of land and destroy whole towns. Floods have forced people to flee their homes, or isolated them when roads were underwater and they couldn't get to the grocery store.

There are economic reasons to store food. Gas is expensive and getting higher almost by the day. Every trip to the store costs more than 3 times what it did 10 years ago.

If you don't have to go as often, you're saving money, and that money can be put toward more stores of food.

In the last several years there have been huge numbers of workers laid off. Unemployment checks are usually not enough to keep a person's bills paid, let alone buy groceries. If it happens to you and you have some basic food stored, you can greatly increase your comfort and lessen the financial strain.

Again, there are safety nets for people who find themselves in that position, but it can take time to complete the application process and begin receiving assistance. At the very least it's good to have enough food to carry you through those first few weeks.

It's a personal decision how much food you think you would feel comfortable storing. By the time you finish reading this book you'll be able to formulate a plan of your own.

Chapter 2

Freeing up money

A lot of people don't like this subject, because it means changing a few things about how and when they spend money! No, I'm not going to tell you to give up all your treats! There's just a few painless tweaks that could make all the difference!

Obviously, if you're eating out a lot, going to the movies, or buying new clothes every month, you know where you can make some cuts. But what if you already don't eat out, go to movies, or buy new clothes?

And what if you already work hard to buy things on sale or use coupons, and your pantry is still pretty empty by the next payday?

The first thing to do is look at everything you spend money on and see if there's a way you can do things cheaper. Even if you can only free up $10 a month you can build up a store of food within a few months. It won't be enough to survive on by itself for longer than a few weeks, but it's the first step, and for some it may be enough.

How can you free up $10 a month? First you can look at things like your cell phone plan, or cable/satellite package, and see if there's anything you can cut without penalty that would save $10 a month. If not, let's see where else you might save.

Can you cut down your transportation costs? Are you close enough to walk or ride a bicycle to work, or to the grocery store or any place you regularly drive? Even just one or two days a week? Depending how far it is and the fuel efficiency (or lack of!) of your vehicle, it might not be hard to save $10 from your fuel costs.

Pack your own lunch and snacks from home, and save money on eating out. My husband used to spend a couple dollars a day on snacks when he went to work. It didn't seem like much until one day he added it up. $2 a day was $10 a week, and approximately $40 a month. Over a year, it was around $500. Even at the current price of things, that would buy a 25-lb. bag of flour, plus a 25-lb. bag of sugar, plus either a 50-lb. bag of rice or a 25-lb. bag of pinto beans, EACH MONTH!

That's just by dropping the $2 a day on snacks! Imagine if you're spending $5 a day

on lunch at a fast-food or other place!
$20/week, $80/month, $960 a year!

What about your utilities? Can you lower
the temperature of your hot water heater?
Wash laundry in cold water? Lower the
thermostat in winter, or raise it in summer?
Turn lights off, use outlet strips for things
like TV and Computer equipment and keep
them turned off when not in use? Many
televisions and other appliances have
circuitry that draws power even when the
appliance is off.

Can you hang your laundry instead of
putting it in the clothes dryer? We saved
almost $15 a month when we stopped using
our dryer. You can put shirts on hangers
and hang them from curtain rods or the
shower rod, drape them over kitchen chairs,
etc. Hang underwear on door knobs or
cabinet knobs. Hang socks over chairs,
curtain rods, etc. If you hang them at bed
time they'll be dry by morning and they
won't be in anyone's way. The smell from
the laundry soap can be pleasant in the air.

Cut back on the amount of soaps you use,
on everything from dishes to laundry to
yourself. The savings will add up when you
don't have to buy these things as often.

Don't mow your lawn until you have to. Mowing less often equals paying less for gas over the summer. Some places have rules about how tall the grass can get, so keep that in mind. Wash your car yourself instead of taking it to a car wash.

Just doing one of these things can free up enough for you to get started buying food storage. Like I said in the introduction, you can prep with only $20 per month, or even $10.

Throw your spare change into a jar and use it for purchasing food.   Even if you only have 50 cents extra each month, that could buy you something such as a can of salt, which is about a pound and a half of salt. I know what you're thinking. Salt? What would I do with all that salt? We'll cover that in the Salt chapter! Well, okay, it's a sub-chapter of Chapter 6!

Chapter 3

Don't Obsess with Nutrition

Some people spend a lot time evaluating nutritional charts and figuring how much of each vitamin or mineral or other nutrient will be needed per person per day. They figure out daily calorie counts per person, based on weight, age, sex, and activity level. They go online and compare prices and ounces at preparedness supply websites.

To me, that's thinking too hard, especially if you're doing good just to scrape together some nickels to get a few things stored up. The stress of worrying about this is probably taxing your health more than a few days or a few weeks eating a sub-standard diet.

The important thing is to at least have some food to handle a short-term emergency. If the power is out for a week after a devastating ice storm, you're going to emerge in fine shape after eating pop tarts and crackers for the duration, unless you have a health issue such as diabetes.

If the power going out from something major such as an EMP and won't be back for months, years, or maybe never, then you'll need to consider other options beyond the pop tarts and crackers. In later chapters we'll not only talk about what to store, but how to supplement it to stretch your supplies.

Most of the things you'll buy as a poverty preppers are basics. They're things like flour, which can be used to make a number of things that you will, hopefully, be able to use along with those things you supplemented your supplies with. That might be vegetables from a garden, or wild berries from the woods, or fish from a nearby stream.

If funds are short, the best plan is to acquire those basic foods you won't be able to grow, forage, hunt, or fish for. You can grow potatoes, carrots, and lettuce, as well as many other vegetables, but you probably can't grow flour, sugar, or rice.

Even if you have the money to buy storage food according to nutrition charts, consider this. Some of the food sold as emergency storage food is unfamiliar to a lot of people. If you go that route, be sure to sample some of it in "normal" times and make sure you and your family will actually eat it.

Try not to fall into the trap of thinking "Oh, if they're hungry enough, my husband and kids WILL eat it!" Sure, they might ... but then they might not! Children will sometimes absolutely refuse to eat unfamiliar foods no matter how hungry they are. Or they may all gripe and complain so much you'll throw everything away and let them starve!!!!

Consider the transition time after a disaster or other emergency. There will be a lot of stress going around just from the shock of whatever has happened. It's not a good time to impose a completely different way of eating onto people going through that.

At least store some things everyone is used to, including treats. It can be things like chips, candy bars, marshmallows, or drinks like pop or kool-aid.

Again, don't get hung up on the nutritional value and calorie counts for short-term emergency food storage. We aren't going for a specific goal, we're just trying to buy what we can, to have something, anything, to eat in a time of need. For people who can barely afford groceries for today, it's more important that they buy the foods they can afford, rather than have nothing stored

because they can't afford 'real' storage
foods.

Chapter 4

Buy what you eat, and rotate it.

In the prepper world there's a saying: Buy what you eat, and eat what you buy. It's good advice. If your family doesn't like beans, or you don't like oatmeal, then don't store it. Don't feel pressured to buy whole wheat and a grinder, if your family doesn't like whole wheat.

This is especially important for the Poverty Prepper, and even more important if you're just starting to build up food storage. Spend what money you have to buy foods you're familiar with, and that you and your family like. Later, when you've stored enough to feel comfortable branching out, then you can add more variety or experiment with new foods.

If you start thinking "well, maybe I should get a bag of whole wheat", then you're going to realize you'll need a wheat grinder. So you'll start looking at reviews and discussions and then it gets complicated. Everyone has different suggestions or opinions. So what happens? You stall and try to make sense of it, and ultimately, you don't buy the wheat or the grinder.

Not to mention that people new to prepping might not want the challenge of finding a place to buy wheat, or to scrounge up money for a grinder.. Rather than push people into foods and equipment they're not familiar with, I prefer to see them get started in a simple way with readily-available, cheap basic food items.

Some people haven't cooked from scratch in a long time, if ever, and just buying a bag of flour will be a big deal for them. They don't need to have the added stress of being told storing flour is bad, that they need whole wheat and a grinder. Someday they might be in a position to buy the wheat and the grinder, but if not, it's okay.

If you need to learn how to cook using ingredients like flour and spices, this is the time to start getting some information about it. There are great websites such as www.allrecipes.com and www.food.com which not only have recipes for everything you can think of, but great easy-to-follow directions.

We're always told to cook from scratch to save money, but if your kitchen isn't well-stocked with the ingredients to do so, your set-up costs and shopping lists will be high. If you continue eating your normal way while stocking up on these basics, eventually you'll have everything you need to cook from scratch without buying it all at once and needing a lot of cash to do it. You can ease into it.

In the short term these foods are adequate in nutrition. In fact, many Americans live on these kinds of food as part of everyday life, and might do better than those who must go through the stress of a diet change during an emergency.

In a long-term situation, you can supplement it, but for now, at least get started. Get some extra food in those cupboards or other storage areas so you have *something* to eat in a crisis.

As you build up your supply of emergency food, use the oldest things first and put newer things behind them. This keeps the food rotated so that nothing gets old enough to become rancid or depleted in nutrition.

Chapter 5

How you're going to stock up

So here's the plan to stock up for tomorrow when you can't afford to eat today. You're going to buy one thing each month. Or maybe two things, depending on the price and how much you have. For around $20 a month you can begin to build up a supply of extra food, but it you're really low on funds, even $10 will do it. Most people should be able to spare $10 a month.

For the first month let's say you buy a 25-lb. bag of flour. Around here a 25-lb. bag of flour can be had for $8 to $10 at this time, (winter of 2011/2012)). I won't mention how upset I am that 10 years ago a 25-lb. bag of flour was $3.99. We'll just go ahead and buy the bag of flour.

Suppose you were able to get it for $8.99 and you had $10.00 in your hand for this month's preps. You could buy a 1-lb. can of salt for 50 cents. Or get two and blow the whole remaining dollar! Or just get the one and put the other 50 cents in a jar to start a fund to supplement your food storage money.

If you're working with $20, you could buy double. Get two 25-lb. bags of flour.

The next month take your $10 and buy a couple of 10-lb. bags of sugar. Depending how much they cost, you might have to buy a 10-lb. bag and a 4-lb. bag. If you have $20 to spend, go ahead and get a 25-lb. bag, which is running around $15 right now. You'll have about $5 left. You can add it to the fund in the jar, or buy a few bottles of spices for $1 apiece at places like Dollar Tree.

The third month you can buy beans. If you only have $10, buy as many 1- or 2-lb. bags as you can, and put any extra money in the food fund jar. If you have $20, try to get a 25-lb. bag of beans. We're paying around $15 for 25 lbs. of pinto beans, though I'm sure the price varies. If you have money left... into the fund jar with it.

Any time you have money left, you have the option of either putting it in the jar, or buying spices, salt, or whatever you can squeeze out of the leftover money. Don't forget things like baking soda, vanilla, cornstarch, baking powder, etc. Just one box, can, or jar of those each month, in addition to the main Staple item, will build up a well-stocked pantry in a short time.

The fourth month you should buy rice. If you have $20 and access to a place like Costco you can buy a 50-lb. bag of white rice and have a couple dollars leftover. If you only have $10, buy a few smaller bags of rice.

Even if you eat rice or these other foods regularly right now, these that you're buying with your prep money are extra above your regular shopping. If you need to dip into them and eat them now, then do so. But don't look at the extra food on the shelf as an excuse to overeat!

You don't have to buy these foods in this order. If you think rice is more important than beans, buy that first and put the beans off for another month. Decide what your own preference is. I'd stick to the flour and sugar the first two months, but it's up to you what you want to do. I could live on just those two basics plus salt, supplemented with garden and forage goods!

I don't consider the basics to be potential barter goods. They're too essential to the survival of myself and my family.

We could come up with more basics, and the little extras to buy with any leftover money, but I think you're getting the idea. Remember what I said about buying what your family will eat. If they've never tried it, buy a small amount and prepare it a few different ways to see if it can be added to your storage plan.

When you've built up a supply of emergency food, then you can branch out and start buying things like powdered milk. You may never want to mix it up and drink it, but if times get tough it's nice to have powdered milk to add to cooked or baked foods, or even to make things like pudding. After a few weeks on tight rations it'll taste pretty good!

Again, you'll be buying what you can squeeze out of that month's money, and it might not stretch far. But see if you can fit it in your budget a couple times a year. Cooking oil and shortening are other foods you should add as time goes by.

There's a glaringly obvious lack of essential foods like fruits and vegetables. That's partly because I'm assuming people in most locations can supplement the flour, beans, rice, and sugar with their own home-grown fruits and veggies, or foraged foods. I'll cover that later in this book.

If you know you won't have any fruits or vegetables immediately available in a crisis, then use the small amounts of leftover money each month to buy the cheapest cans of them that you can afford. Even just a couple a month will add up, and you can supplement your basics with them if you need to eat out of your storage.

Some areas have case lot sales, and if one comes along, use that month's money to buy a case or two of a vegetable or fruit your family likes.

It's possible that you will be able to barter some of your basics with friends or neighbors for fruits or vegetables when the need arises. If you've bought a bunch of those $1 bottles of spices from dollar stores, you might very well be the only one in the neighborhood who still has garlic salt, cinnamon, chili powder, and other spices that enhance the culinary experience! Their value will increase many times over what you paid for them!

Do the same with those 1½-lb. cans of salt I recommended you start stocking up on!

Don't barter the whole can! Measure some out into something smaller, like an empty and washed/dried vitamin bottle, and trade it for a half a dozen tomatoes from a neighbor's garden, or a head of lettuce and some carrots.

It's taking a chance, I know, to assume one could work out a barter arrangement, but it's a possibility.

Chapter 6

What to buy and how to use it

In this chapter I'm going to take each of the basics and discuss how to use it. I'm sure you'll think of other ideas, but there are people who won't have any ideas! In this day and age it's not that uncommon to never have used raw ingredients like flour. That's where we'll start!

<u>Flour</u>

What can you do with flour? You can mix it with baking soda and salt, add a little shortening or similar fat, and a little water, and you'll have biscuits. Pancakes are almost the same recipe except you use cooking oil instead of shortening, and eggs and/or sugar if you have them.

Don't have baking powder? Flour, salt, and fat are the basic ingredients for tortillas. That's about as simple as it gets!

You can allow a flour and water mixture to gather natural yeast from the air and it becomes sourdough starter. It helps to have a friend or a book to give you advice about it, but you can experiment too. Then you can make bread without yeast. If you have things like salt or sugar, you can add them to the bread to make them tastier. But it can be done with just flour and water. Just remember that edible doesn't always mean tasty!

It's not hard to make a decent "white sauce" or gravy with just flour and water. Salt and pepper make it appealing, other spices can make it delicious! Bouillon cubes are a great stock-up food (yes, I know, they're full of sodium and usually have MSG in them!) to add to flour gravy. Or just boil up the bones of whatever critter you've raised, hunted, or fished for, and make your "gravy" or sauce with that and flour.

With flour on hand you can whip up simple cakes, muffins, and cookies. If you stumble across wild berries you could use flour to make a crust (Flour, Salt, Fat, and water are the basic recipe) and have a pie.

No pie pan? Tear off pieces of the dough, flatten them with your hands, put some of the fruit on the dough, fold over and crimp the edges. Now you have a bunch of little "personal" pies! If you have sugar, add a little to the fruit if you want. You might even have a can of cinnamon, which means you could sprinkle some of that on the pies!

If you have meat and/or vegetables you could make a pot pie. Mix them with whatever spices you like, or just with salt and pepper, or nothing at all, and make them like fruit pies.

Be creative. If you don't have the right pan for the job, try a different one. If you need recipes, go to the websites I posted above, or do a search on your own. You might already own cookbooks or can get them from the library.

Sugar

You can add sugar to biscuits or bread to make sweet rolls or muffin-type desserts. Fruit cobblers are yummy, and can be made by adding it to the fruit, then making a sweet biscuit dough to put on top.

Even if you don't have pectin you can make fruit syrups by crushing fruit and boiling it, gently, with sugar. A little bit of cornstarch will help thicken it if you're having problems with thickening.

Sugar has been used as a preservative. Sugar inhibits bacterial growth. It's most often used to preserve fruit, but can also be used to preserve meat. If you're interested in learning more about this, search the internet and you'll find a lot of information about it.

Gather wild rose hips, mint leaves, raspberry leaves, or other wild plants for tea, and sweeten with a little bit of sugar. Some people recommend storing honey because it's "healthier", and no doubt it is, but it's also more expensive. Don't feel bad about storing and using sugar.

When gathering wild plants make SURE you know what you are picking. Don't take a chance or eat anything you've had to use guesswork on to identify. It's not worth getting sick, or worse. This is especially true regarding mushrooms.

Rice

Rice is a very versatile food. You can use it in sweet dishes or main course meat or veggie type dishes. You can mix just about anything with it and it'll taste good.

I'm talking about plain white rice. Brown

rice is indeed more nutritious and has fiber, but it's also more expensive and doesn't store as long. The oils in brown rice make it go rancid fairly quickly, unless you can store it in a freezer.

White rice will keep forever if you keep it dry. The 'hows' of storing food like rice will be covered in Chapter 7.

Rice can also be ground into flour. It doesn't have gluten in it, so it doesn't make good yeast-type bread. It's often mixed with other flours, such as potato flour, but can be used by itself.

Here's a pancake recipe from http://allrecipes.com/recipe/rice-flour-pancakes/:

Ingredients

- 3 eggs
- 1/2 cup milk
- 1 tablespoon vegetable oil
- 1/2 teaspoon salt
- 1 cup rice flour

Directions

Beat the eggs in a mixing bowl; stir in the milk, vegetable oil, and salt. Whisk in the rice flour until no dry lumps remain. Cover the bowl and let stand at room temperature for 1 hour or in the refrigerator overnight.

Heat a lightly-oiled griddle over medium-high heat. Drop batter by large spoonfuls onto the griddle and cook until bubbles form and the edges are dry. Flip and cook until browned on the other side. Repeat with remaining batter.

Rice is a soft grain, so it can be ground even with rocks if you don't have a grain grinder. Find a large flat rock with a somewhat smooth surface. Now find another rock, about the size of a soup can, that fits comfortably in your hand. Clean the surfaces you will be using. Put a tablespoon or two of flour on the big rock and grind at it with the other one. You can push, pull, slide, make circles, whatever you want, to grind the rice. You'll figure out your favorite method as you go.

Or just cook the rice as grains. There are so many ways to use rice it's hard to make a list. We cook up a big pan of it and use it for many things over a few days. We might fry some up with eggs, onions, and peppers one morning, with a sprinkle of spices on it, and later in the day mix some rice with fruit and cool whip. For dinner we might make a homemade stew out of garden vegetables and venison, and pour it over rice.

Homemade tortillas are very easy to make, as mentioned in the flour section above.

You can make burritos or enchiladas, and use rice to stretch the meat, cheese, and/or beans you put inside them. Or you can make them like Hot Pockets, and put rice in along with meat, cheese, and/or vegetables.

Another delicious idea is to mix rice with pie filling or even jam or jelly, and roll it inside tortillas or crepes. Crepes are thin, sweet pancakes that can be rolled around a filling much like a tortilla.

My husband's take on the whole thing is that he would store rice before he would store flour. He said he can cook up rice and add it to everything, such as vegetables from the garden or woods, and "a couple of squirrels". He would need recipes to make things with the flour.

If your line of thinking goes along with that idea, then buy rice first, and store more of it than flour.

Beans

Some people don't like beans, and others don't care for the flatulent side effect of beans. However, beans are one of the cheapest and easiest to store proteins. Like white flour, white sugar, and white rice, dry beans will keep for a very long time if kept dry.

Beans do have an exception to their storage life. After about ten years or so they reach the point where they will need more cooking time. We cooked some red beans that were 25 years old and they never did truly get soft. They were soft enough to chew but had a grainy texture.

Some beans cook faster than others. White beans cook pretty fast compared to red and pinto beans. That might not be an issue, but if it is, then look for beans with shorter cooking time. It saves resources, such as the gas, electricity, or whatever you cook with.

I know of two ways to cook beans. One way is to soak them in water over night, drain and rinse them, then add more water and let them simmer for a few hours. The other way, which I learned because of all the times I forgot to soak the beans, is to boil them for 2 minutes, remove them from the heat for an hour, then simmer for a few hours.

Beans can be a side dish, or made into things like chili, baked beans, beans & dumplings, burritos, and dozens of other meals, depending on the type of bean. We usually see baked beans made with white beans, and chili made with red beans, but there's no rule about it!

In some ways beans are like rice. You can add meat, cheese, vegetables, or spices to them and create different meals. I can't think of any fruits that would be appealing to add to beans, unless one considers tomatoes a fruit, which botanically speaking, they are a fruit.

Leftover beans can be mashed and fried as Refried beans. You can add onions and garlic to them, or just salt and pepper. A little bit of Salsa is interesting stirred into them! If you have it, you could sprinkle shredded cheese on top when you eat it. Cheese is a luxury in our poverty cuisine, and used sparingly and with appreciation!

If you really don't like beans and expect to have other sources of protein, such as wild game or fish, then drop beans from your storage plan.

Salt

Salt is and isn't a basic. You can live without it, since most foods have enough natural sodium in them to keep you healthy, but it's sure nice to have. If you're working hard and sweating a lot, then it becomes more important to have additional salt. I don't get real hung up on electrolyte balance, but I try to make sure that we're getting sodium and sugar as well as water when we're working hard.

Salt is very cheap. Last time I looked it was still 50 cents or less for store-brand salt in a 1-lb. cardboard can. Costco has a 25-lb. bag for around $3, but a person who is truly a poverty prepper probably doesn't have a Costco card. So unless you know someone who will buy you a bag as a gift (and you should be kind and reciprocate, perhaps make a cash donation to them! Lol), you're pretty much stuck buying the 1-lb. Cans.

You can buy pickling salt in bigger containers but check the price per pound. It's the same salt as table salt, only it's coarser (larger grains).

If others in your area are also hit by whatever has caused you to be eating from your emergency rations, it's a good bet you'll eventually be able to barter that salt for other foods or goods.

Other Basics

If you hit the big time and want to buy things like macaroni, coffee, and cocoa powder, then by all means, go ahead and do so. But before you add variety to your storage, consider these two, probably-should-also-be-basic, food items.

Powdered milk is a good food to put on your list after you've gotten some of the main staples put aside. If you're concerned about a long-term situation of hard times, it can add calcium, protein, and small amounts of other nutrients to your diet.

If you have children in your household, powdered milk is something you probably want to include as you begin. In that case, put it into your monthly rotation of foods to buy.

Young children will often drink powdered milk without complaining. It's harder for older people who are used to fresh milk. People of all ages don't usually notice the powdered milk when it's mixed into cooked or baked foods, such as desserts or casseroles.

A lot of recipes that call for milk can be

made with water instead. I make cake, biscuits, and pancakes with no milk, and they come out fine. Some things like pudding can't be made by replacing the milk with water, but gravy can be made with water instead of milk.

When I'm baking with powdered milk I don't usually mix up the milk and add it to the recipe. You can do that, but I find it faster to just add the dry milk powder to the dry ingredients, then add the amount of water I would have used to mix the milk, to the wet ingredients.

Cooking oils and shortening are the last item I would consider a "basic". Many of the meal ideas I've written about are better with oil or shortening, and some are hard to make without them. They also add calories and fat to your diet, which will be important on a lean diet of emergency foods.

Plus, you will probably be more physically active since you might be walking everywhere instead of driving, or doing labor such as sawing limbs from fallen trees after a storm or hurricane, to clear debris. Or you might be sawing it because you need firewood for heat. You might be out with a shovel and hoe starting a garden.

This isn't the time to be picky. If every penny counts, buy what's cheap. In good times we might prefer extra-virgin olive oil and coconut oil, but if we're broke and we're preparing for even harder times, get the store-brand vegetable oil and the store-brand unhealthy partially-hydrogenated shortening, or better yet, a can of lard. Lard is at least one step better than regular shortening, unless you're a vegetarian.

Storing oil and shortening is a tricky thing. They go rancid fairly quickly. Your oil should never just be sitting on a counter by the stove unless you go through a bottle a week. Even then a dark cupboard is better. Light is the enemy of oil.

I know this isn't the chapter on how to store oil, but this is so important that I don't want it to get buried in paragraphs about buckets, jars, bottles, etc., and places to put them.

Whenever possible, buy cooking oil in glass jars. Tinted glass jars are even better. Unfortunately, that's not likely with cheap oils. You'll probably end up with plastic bottles. If you have glass jars at home you could transfer the oil to those for storage. I've done that with both oil and shortening.

The best place to store oils is a dark, cool place with a steady temperature. A garage or shed might be cold at night or most of the winter, but a sunny day will raise the temperature, then the night will drop it again. That's hard on all foods, but more so on oils or high-fat foods.

If you have to store oils/shortening in a place like that, place it close to the floor, preferably on the north side of the building, and try to bury it with other boxes, or cover with layers of newspapers or old blankets, or anything that will help insulate it and keep it at a steady temperature.

Make sure you rotate the oil and shortening to keep the freshest stuff you can on hand. If things really fall apart and what you've stored is all you have left, you don't want to have eaten up the newest bottle you bought, and have one in the garage that is a year and a half old. It's probably still good, but don't take the chance. Use up the oldest one first. Rancid oil isn't pleasant and it's not healthy for you.

I know we've been through my ideas about nutrition and poverty prepping, but the type of "not healthy" for you regarding rancid oils has more to do with it's potential to harm your liver and other ill-effects. It's not like being a little short of one vitamin or another occasionally.

Chapter 7

Creative ways to store it

Since we just talked about how to store oils and shortening, let's move right in to talking about how to actually store your food.

What to store it in

Mylar bags, oxygen absorbers, and hermetically sealed 5-gallon buckets, right? Wrong! Not on MY budget!

The 'Cadillac' of my food storing containers are 2-gallon buckets from the grocery store bakery! They give them away here, but a lot of places charge for them. In my opinion it's worth the dollar or two to acquire some of these.

I also like the smaller size. They're lighter and that means easier for me to carry around. They fit in smaller places where 5-gallon buckets don't fit.

The ones I get have an air-tight and water-tight seal. I've filled them with water and shook them, turned them upside down and let them sit, and nothing leaks out. When they're good and dry, I put my food item or items in them.

The first thing to do is to make sure you have the bucket and the food to be stored sitting in the same room for a few hours to equalize the temperature. When you put the food in the bucket, tap on the sides now and then to help the food pack and settle. You'll not only fit more in the bucket this way, but you'll also reduce the amount of air/oxygen left in the bucket when you put the lid on.

When I've packed as much of the food item into the bucket as I can, I lay the lid on top and put one knee on it. As I snap the lid shut all the way around, my knee is forcing out as much air as possible. It almost creates a bit of a vacuum in the bucket once it's sealed.

I have a friend who just can't leave it there. She wants to seal it more. She puts caulk around the seam where the bucket and lid come together. When she first asked me how else she could seal the buckets I had recommended the old stand-by: Duct tape!

I just close the buckets and leave it at that. My poverty prepping involves a pretty steady turnover, but if someday I'm able to have enough backed up to last longer, I might look into whether I should caulk or otherwise seal my buckets!

Then I take a 'sharpie' marker and label the bucket. So, how do you do this? Write it on the top? NO!!!! When they're stacked you can't see what it says if it's written on the lid!

Oh! Write it on the SIDE!!! Well, sort of. Not just on the middle of the side though. If you do that, you might rub it off handling the bucket. There are usually ridges under where the lid goes on, and the handle attaches somewhere in that zone. I write in the space between the ridges, where fingers will probably never touch.

I put something like this: White Flour, 3/2012. After I use up that bucket I scrub off the writing so I'm ready to re-label it with the name and date of whatever goes into it next. Often it's another bag of the same item, and I just have to change the date.

Be careful about buckets. Make sure they're food grade. I've heard of people buying buckets from Home Building supply stores and putting food in them. I've also heard of people buying the empty-but-new paint cans to store food in. I doubt those are food-safe either.

If you must use a bucket that might not be food safe, at least put the food in a food-safe plastic bag. NOT garbage bags! Something like old bread bags or produce bags. The bags they put your groceries in at the store are not air-tight, so don't use those.

If you can afford mylar bags, they might keep your food safe in a questionable bucket. But if you can afford Mylar bags, you can afford to skip those and buy food-grade buckets. First ask around at the grocery stores and bakeries in your area and see if someone has free buckets.

I stumbled onto another source of buckets recently. Some of our neighbors are custodians at the school, and they get buckets from the cafeteria! You might want to ask, if you're looking for a source of buckets.

Restaurants are another possibility. Sometimes instead of buckets you can get gallon jugs with wide tops that held mayonnaise or pickles. You can also ask at convenience stores that have a deli/snack counter. One time I got a bunch of large containers that had held potato salad and other salads.

Heavy plastic juice bottles can be used, but if they're clear you'll want to store them inside a box to keep them dark, or in a cabinet, under a bed, in a closet, or other dark place.

Containers that don't make good storage containers are things like milk jugs. The plastic become brittle in a relatively short time. This could lead to cracking and breaking, which could spill your food, or allow moisture or bugs to get into it.

If you must use milk jugs, wash them out good and make sure they're dry, and I mean make SURE you let them sit until they're good and dry!!! Then store them in a place as far removed from the elements (sun, wind, light, rain) as possible. It might help to set them inside a plastic bag or two, to reduce oxidation of the jug's plastic.

Glass jars from salsa, pickles, jams and jellies, and other foods might not hold a lot, but they're good containers. You can use them for your smaller storage items, like salt and spices. Most cheap spices will come in plastic jars, but salt usually comes in a cardboard can. Get it out of there and into glass jars so dampness or water won't damage it. You can set the whole cans into a bucket and keep adding them until the bucket is full, if you'd rather store them that way.

The small glass jars are easy to tuck here and there, so they might be good for your salt. Plus, if it comes to having to barter some of it away, you can hunt around and find a jar, and not let on how much salt you have tucked away!

Where to store it

In a temperature-controlled underground bunker, right? I think you're on to me now! I tuck things anywhere I can, but I try to keep the "dark, cool, steady temperature" rule in mind.

Good places around the house that come quickly to mind are under the beds, under and behind furniture, and even right in sight as PART of the furniture! I've seen people stack boxes of canned goods, lay a piece of plywood or paneling on top to make a hard surface, and put a table cloth over it. Then they set a lamp on it and have an "end table". You can make a "coffee table" the same way.

Bags of flour, sugar, etc., can be put in boxes too, not just cans and jars. If you need to fill corners, stick crumpled newspaper, like those free Thrifty nickel type newspapers (since we're poverty here, we don't want to spend money if we don't have to!) in there.

Let's take a break for a little humor here. Take those free newspapers….they're good for SO much! If you need to start a fire later on when times are hard, like maybe in the backyard (or on the balcony of your apartment), you have paper to start it with! If you need something to occupy your mind, you can un-crumple and read them!

They can be educational…you can read them to your grandkids someday and talk about how the world used to be! Or sit around with your friends and buddies and laugh about the 'good old days'!

You can use them for toilet paper. A tip about that or any paper, such as phone books, is to tear off the size of paper you think you'll need, crumple it good, then straighten it back out. That breaks down the paper fibers and makes it more comfortable for the business at hand, plus makes it more absorbent.

Okay, back to where to store your food. Salt in small jars, spice bottles, and other small food containers can be slid under your couch or living room chairs. You can look for spaces behind or above overhead cabinets. I saw a bathroom once where the homeowner had jars of spices on top of the mirror cabinet. They were packed tightly, one next to the other, and there were dozens of them.

A decorative towel with lace edges was spread over it. You had to lift it to see that there were spices there. I didn't. My friend did, to show me!

Do you have a linen closet in the hallway? See if there's room behind the piles of folded towels for small containers and jars.

Large containers and buckets are harder, especially for apartment dwellers. You can use the obvious spaces, like closets and under the kitchen sink. But ultimately you won't have as many places to use. Don't give up on it though. Perhaps you can start with smaller containers, even for flour and sugar. The important thing is the food, not the size of the container.

For those with basements, garages, and sheds, you have more options. Try to avoid attics or the rafters and loft space of garages and sheds. They have too much temperature swing. If that's ALL you have, then use that space, but rotate often, and don't plan on long-term food storage up there for most items.

Sugar and salt are the two foods that can withstand extremes of heat and cold. If your only storage place fits those conditions, then go heavy on sugar and salt, and plan to barter for other things.

Even if you're the only one having a hard time, you can probably find someone who will trade some vegetables for sugar or salt, especially if you have good friends. They'll want to help you, and they'll appreciate that you're coming to them with something and not just asking for a hand-out. It'll feel weird, but you'll be ahead of the rest in the learning curve about bartering if bad times spread to everyone else!

Some people talk about caching supplies.

Caching, to me, means burying them. I've read a lot about it and talked to those who have done it, and there's a lot that can go wrong. Buried buckets have been known to leak, or get cracked from movement of the earth, which can be from normal activities of traffic nearby or something bigger like an earthquake.

If you're going to bury food or other supplies, use extreme measures to seal your container. Make sure you won't come back to dig it up and find a Wal-mart built over it!

Chapter 8

Stretching it!

Okay, you've got some basic food storage and it's all packed away in containers and resting comfortably in it's storage places. You're bopping along through life and SPLAT! just like that, you get the pink slip. You apply for unemployment and get a lot of exercise pounding the street looking for a new job.

If you're lucky, you'll be able to keep your place of residence, be that a rental or a home you're buying. If you're even luckier you already own it, mortgage-free.

But you won't have enough money to buy food, and standing in the line at the soup kitchen doesn't appeal to you... yet! Time to start stretching your supplies. Cutting back on how much you eat will only help to some extent. If you've followed my suggestions, you don't have the foods on hand for a decent balanced diet.

Like I said back at the beginning of this book, if you're only eating out of your emergency supplies for a short-term situation, such as a major weather event, nutrition isn't a big concern. But if you're laid off, or something terrible happens to our country and/or the world, then nutrition will become an issue.

Gardening

If you've never gardened, now would be a good time to pick up some basic knowledge of it. You can do this by starting a garden, hanging around (and offering to help!!!) someone who has a garden, read books about it, watch you tube-videos about growing fruit and vegetables, or buy seed packets and hope the little directions on the back will teach you how to grow them!

Starting a garden now while your life doesn't depend on it is better than waiting until it does. Don't tell me you don't have space for a garden, or your soil is too poor, or any other excuse! You can grow things in containers, and soil can be improved.

I could go on at length about the many sizes and types of containers you can use, but there are dozens of books and you-tube videos for you to learn about container gardening. Basically, anything that will hold dirt can grow something. You can take a vitamin bottle and scoop some dirt into it, and plant a radish seed. Or better yet, a dozen of them! Radishes are fast-growing. In about a month you'll have a ready-to-eat radish.

One radish? Don't laugh. Everything helps! Take a cottage cheese carton and plant some romaine lettuce! Cut the top part of a milk jug off, down to the top of the handle, and plant carrots. Or plant a wedge of potato with at least one eye on it, and you could get a plant with half a dozen or more potatoes down in the dirt.

Onions grow well in containers, both the bulb type and the "green onions". So does celery, and if you like celery you're in for a real treat with home-grown celery! Most of these things don't depend on pollination by bees.

If you have space for an outdoor garden you'll be able to grow a wide variety of food. The types of things you can grow depends, at least in part, on how hot or cold it is, how humid or dry, and how much rain or wind you get. All of those things can be worked with, and you'll learn those things as you go along.

For instance, if it's going to frost before your harvest, you can cover your plants with old sheets and blankets, or even newspaper (like those free newspapers we already talked about), to keep the frost from killing your plants. If it's hot and dry, you can mulch around the bottoms of your plants with dry grass or leaves, straw, bark chips, gravel, or free newspapers, to protect the roots from burning up.

When the soil dries out and feels crumbly, water your plants. Water deeply, and less often, so the plant will send roots down to look for moisture. Daily watering will keep the roots shallow and a dry spell can kill them.

If the wind howls where you live, find something to make a barrier. You can pound sticks into the ground and tie blankets or sheets or tarps along it to divert the wind away from your plants. Wind can break or dry out your plants. Most places don't have wind to that extreme.

You can eat your harvests as you go, or slice and dehydrate them on cookie sheets, freeze them, or can them. If you need to learn how to do those things the same advice applies: Find someone to teach you, read about it, or watch you-tube videos. Another source of knowledge is internet forums where they discuss such things as gardening and preserving the harvest.

Foraging

There is a wide variety of fruits, nuts, vegetables, roots, mushrooms, and herbs just about everywhere, whether you live in the city or the country. The most important thing you MUST do is to learn to identify the plant beyond all doubt.

If possible, find a mentor to teach you. There are classes you can take, but this costs money not only to attend them, but to travel to and from the classes, unless you can walk or ride your bicycle to them.

Books can be tricky, since the pictures will usually show one example of the plant, and often in only one or two stages of it's growth. Sometimes they just have sketches, which confound me!

Videos are a good possibility because you'll have a knowledgeable person (hopefully) who shows you the plant and talks about it. However you learn, make absolutely sure you are harvesting the right plant. If you are doing this alone, keep careful notes so if you get sick, someone can figure out what caused it.

I'm not trying to be scary. I've been foraging for years and so far I've been lucky. But there are a few plants that look so much alike that I leave them alone, because the one that isn't the plant I would want is a deadly one. I'm not hungry enough to take that chance, especially when there are so many other edibles all around us.

There isn't a lot of calories or fat in most foraged foods, with the exception of nuts. That's why I consider foraging to be a *supplement* to my stored basics.

Even if you're in the city, look around you! On the ground you'll probably find dandelion, pineapple weed (relative of Chamomile), plantain (White man's foot), clover, roses (all are edible), wild mustard, wild onions and chives, and dozens of others.

Clover, for example, can be eaten in salads, or dried and ground into flour. White clover, dried and ground, was used to extend wheat flour during the potato famine in

Ireland. At the base of a head of purple clover there is a drop of moisture that tastes like honey. What a treat that would be if you didn't have any sugar! But you do, because you stocked the basics! ☺

Rose flowers are edible and very decorative in a salad. A surprising variety of flowers are edible for humans, and that might be something for you to research if you like salads.

A lot of fruit and nut trees planted years ago are now neglected by the current owners. If you see fruits and nuts falling to the ground and not being picked up, consider knocking on the door and asking if you can have some of it. Use safety precautions when approaching the home of someone you don't know.

Take someone with you, if possible, and have them stand back on the sidewalk so whoever answers the door knows they can't just grab you and drag you inside. There's a witness out there.

The question I just ask the owner is if I can clean up the "windfalls" on the ground. Most people are happy not to have to mow over them or pick them up themselves. And a lot of the people I've asked have said to please take all of it if I want.

I was cleaning up a peach tree once and the homeowner came out to chat. I asked why they didn't use the peaches themselves, and the lady told me they might be buggy because they haven't been sprayed, and that they're not government inspected. She said the ones from the store are safer.

I didn't argue with her. I boxed up all those organic peaches that weren't buggy, although some were bruised from falling of the tree, and took them home and canned them. I just cut off the bad spots.

Nut trees are the same. It seems a lot of people don't want to go to the trouble to pick up the nuts, take off the husks, shell them, roast them, and eat them. Okay, that works out good for me! Because I WILL take the time to do all that!

We have wild strawberry and wild grape plants all over our property, along with kinnikinnik berries (sort of a bland cranberry) and service berries (a bland blueberry). The strawberries are small but very sweet, and in a short time we can pick enough to add to pancakes or muffins. The grapes are so sour they'll turn your face inside out, but they make great jelly!

The kinnikinniks can be used to stretch cranberries, and the service berries make a decent pie by themselves, or can be mixed with the wild huckleberries that we pick farther up on the mountain.

We've lived in places where blackberries went to waste by the truckload, all over hillsides and roadsides and throughout the national forest. What a shame! Those are organic berries full of resveratrol and anti-oxidants, as well as vitamin C!

Speaking of Vitamin C, after rose petals fall off the plant, the rose hip forms, and it's very high in Vitamin C. You can make tea with it, and it makes a decent jelly. You can also just eat them, but some people like to remove the hairy seeds inside first. Cut them in half and use the tip of your knife to nudge the seeds out.

Pine needles are high in Vitamin C, and pine needle tea is something of a health fad right now.

These are just a few of the wonderful free foods waiting for you to start foraging for.

Why wait until times are hard, or an emergency happens, to supplement your current diet! Then you'll know all about it when you need it, plus... maybe you can barter that knowledge for something different to eat, by teaching someone else how to forage!

Fishing

Take some of that extra change you saved in your storage fund jar, and buy a cheap roll of fishing line and a few hooks. That's pretty basic, but if you don't already fish and don't know anyone who does, then this is where you start.

If you're a little better off, get a cheap $10 fishing rod and reel combo from Wal-mart. They might be more now, but that's how much they were a few years ago.

Don't worry about all those lures and cool things they sell for fishing. If you've got to have them, go easy on them until you learn more about fishing and which ones really do work for the fish in your area.

You might want to pick up some of those little weights to hold the hook and line in the water.

I go fishing with my husband and enjoy it, but I don't have much technical knowledge. I fish with my $10 combo and a few little lures that I thought were "cute". Sometimes I dig worms in my garden, or we use corn. We mostly catch Pike and Perch in the lake near our house, and I do almost as good as my husband. Neither of us catch many fish!

However, we do go out and fish, and I'm going to take my own advice and start reading up on it and watch some you-tubes and see if I can increase my skill! Or I can pick the brains of our son and one of our son-in-laws who fish fanatically, and catch fish when no one else does!

I've kind of coasted along on the fishing thing, knowing others in the family have the knowledge, skill, and hours of experience. That's not a good thing. I might not need to become as proficient as they are, but I have the opportunity to learn more, and I should.

Hunting

This is a complex subject. I think we spend more on licenses to hunt than it would have cost to buy the meat, pound for pound. However, our family enjoys hunting, and we like the organic meat from the woods. I like knowing the meat I eat came from an animal that never knew confinement.

They lived in their wild and natural home clear up to the moment of death, which is at our own hand, and hopefully happens as quickly as possible so the animal doesn't suffer.

I like knowing my meat didn't stand around in a feedlot being fed and injected with who knows what, and knowing that I had the courage to kill it myself (or a member of my family did), and that I didn't rely on a stranger I'll never see to do my dirty work.

But like I said, we pay for licenses. We had to buy rifles and ammunition. Other costs to consider are fuel to drive to places to hunt, and in some cases, for lodging and meals. In 'normal' times, hunting is a sport or pleasant past time, rather than for survival, for most people.

Unless the world has totally fallen apart and there is no government left, which I consider highly unlikely, you MUST obey the hunting laws. The only exception is a very rare situation when you perhaps survived a plane crash and you've spent weeks waiting to be rescued, and you need food. Even then, I'm not absolutely sure on this.

So, if you're a poverty prepper and you want to hunt to supplement your basic storage, figure up the costs and then decide. Small game might be a better meat option. In some states, rabbits and squirrels can be hunted without a license.

You can learn how to set snares and traps for small game, and I know for sure there are good you-tube videos about this on the internet!

Raising your own animals

This is not a practical option for most people. It takes space to raise them, and a means to feed them. The cost of animal feed is likely to be more than it's worth to raise the animal, and on a low budget, it's something to consider. In addition, you may have other costs such as fencing, housing, and keeping the animal(s) healthy.

Will you be able to kill and butcher the animal when the time comes? How will you preserve the meat? Where will you dispose of the "guts", bones, and hide of the animal(s)?

If you have never had meat animals before, you could start with something small and easy-to-feed like rabbits. Even on a small piece of land in a cold climate you can grow and gather enough to keep rabbits fed. They'll eat grains, vegetables, fruits, grasses, willow and other tender branches. You can make a portable cage and just move it around the yard periodically and let it forage. Rabbits need more than grass, though, so if your yard isn't covered with nutritious plants like dandelions and clover, you'll have to supplement with other foods. I used to take my pruners and snip off the occasional willow or aspen branch and toss it in to my rabbits.

There is much you'll need to learn about how many cages you'll need and how to manage your rabbits. The same is true of any meat animals you want to raise. Many people reading this book already have or have had domestic meat animals, but for those who haven't and don't, please do some research before you tackle this.

Bartering

A lot of people talk about bartering as a post-apocalyptic kind of thing, but it's something that can help now, too. Remember the salt and spices I recommended you pick up with the small change left after buying your basics each month? Those are one thing you have to barter with. It might be hard to find takers unless something big happens, but keep in mind the friends who want to help you out!

I know, that's kind of lame. So what can you barter while your times are hard but most people's aren't? How about foraged foods? Fruit, berries, nuts, and things like that. Or, tied in with bartering, have you thought about taking those things to a Farmer's market and selling them?

If you find homeowners who will let you pick the fruit or nuts off their trees, preserve some for yourself, and try to sell or barter the rest. Our farmer's market lets us barter, but we have to report the value of what we could have sold it for. I still come out ahead.

Herbs are another good one to gather and sell or barter. Funny how many people won't go pick rose hips or pineapple weed and dry them for their own use, but they'll buy it from me at the Farmer's market after I do those things!

One of the hottest things I had going at the Farmer's market was dried huckleberries! I picked a few gallons of berries, dried them, and bagged them in those small snack-size ziplock bags, and sold them for $3 apiece. That's $3 for about a handful! Not only did I sell everyone of them, but it didn't cost me anything to get there. I rode my bicycle 16 miles to the Farmer's Market! Win-win for this poverty prepper!

Not all the dried berries were cash sales. I went home with organic green peppers, zucchini (hey! I like it!), onions, and a few other things I bartered them for.

If you know how to do something, like foraging for wild foods, you could barter that skill. Maybe trade some walks in the wild on a learning/gathering expedition for some sweet corn from your student's garden. Whatever your job is or was, you might be able to barter that.

We've all heard stories of someone doing the roofing work for another guy, who fixes a car for the first guy, and that sort of thing. We got our first solar panel for our solar electric system when my husband repaired a car for someone. They had bought the panel for Y2K, and we know how Y2K turned out. They had no money and needed a starter put on their car and a few other small repairs, and they had the panel sitting around.

We live off-grid and used oil lamps for light for several years. With the solar panel and an old car battery, we were in business for having a few 'real' lights in our cabin!

Is there stuff you have sitting around that you've tried to sell, and because of the poor economy or other reasons, it didn't sell? Offer it for sale or TRADE! Say "make offer". Write it up on a piece of paper, neatly, and post it on free bulletin boards.

If there's something you really need, ask around but make it clear you have to barter for it. Or put up a free notice in the same way as the above paragraph: "Needed: hammer and nails. Will trade nice suit, lightly worn, size whatever", or whatever you need and whatever you have to trade.

I hear a lot of anecdotal stories of this working, and it won't cost you anything to try. So give it a chance.

In a true post-apocalyptic world there will be shortages of many foods. A lot of serious preppers with money are stocking up on things like coffee, booze, and cigarettes for trading. Also popular to store as potential barter items are things like matches, lighters, and batteries. Those cost more than the average poverty prepper can put out for barter items that might never be needed.

All that salt and bottles of spices you kept adding to your preps for such small amounts of money will now be useful! I'm amazed how many prepper friends I talk to who haven't even thought about things like spices and salt! You could be sitting on some serious barter wealth!

Bartering, in and of itself, can be a dangerous thing in desperate times. Be careful who you let know what you have. Hungry people do things they wouldn't otherwise do.

Stealing

Gotcha! I would never, ever recommend that. No one is entitled to something that doesn't belong to them, no matter how

hungry or desperate they think they are.
There's always a way, even if you have to
start begging. But please, don't become one
of those who stand by the highway in front
of huge stores with a sign asking for "help"
or money. Approach a church or other
organization first, or your friends or family.
Throw yourself on their mercy if you have
to, and offer whatever you can to them, such
as labor or volunteer work.

But do not steal, and do not expect
something for nothing. Keep your dignity.
Poverty is no excuse for becoming a
scumbag.

Chapter 9

Non-food Items

Once you have some food storage built up, you can watch for sales on non-food items you use. If you see tooth paste on sale for .79, use some of your storage fund money to buy an extra tube. Buy two if you can afford it. Same with Shampoo and other things you use.

But don't go nuts on these things. I've seen people on internet forums arguing about how much toilet paper to store! Some people had hundreds of rolls put away!

I wouldn't store more than about 3 weeks' worth of toilet paper. Most short-term situations will be over by then, and if not, you've got those free newspapers, right?

If it starts as, or turns into, a long-term situation, you've got 3 weeks (more if you have a lot of those free newspapers bundled and stored!) to think of alternatives. Some plants, like mullein, have big soft leaves that work well.

Another alternative is to cut fabric into

squares and use them, with the plan to wash and reuse them. Sounds icky, but it's not that bad. With cloth diapers you have a baby who does the entire job on the cloth. With cloth toilet paper you only have dabs of "stuff" and it washes out easily.

You could set aside one bucket to toss the used ones in, and then wash them in there. Pour water, preferably boiling water, into it, and add soap and/or bleach if you have it, then poke at it with a stick to agitate the cloths. Drain off as much water as you can and add rinse water. Repeat a couple times, then wring them squeezing handfuls at a time, and drape them over tree branches, a fence, or wherever you can. Squares about 6" big are adequate. You can always use a second or third one if necessary.

You could even do this now, and use the money you save by not buying toilet paper, to buy more food preps. There are things that are non-essential but we consider them important. It can be hard to stock up on them if you don't have money, but you can set a goal to buy one thing each month. Review how you spend money and see if you can free up a few more dollars by cutting back somewhere.

Deodorant, shampoo, and other personal care items are nice to have, but expendable. Eating is not. Food is more important than these other things.

Chapter 10

Conclusion

To people who make a lot of money this will all seem ludicrous. The idea of money being so short that a sack of flour could break the bank is foreign to them, but we live with it every day.

I know people who spend more on their truck payment than we even make in a month. I know others (and some are the same people!) who spend more eating out in a week than we spend on groceries over a month.

My heart sinks when I go to the grocery store. I couldn't afford what things used to cost, and prices just keep rising.

I'm sure there are a lot of you out there with just as tight of a budget as we have, and you've been feeling isolated and alone in your frustration, watching the world seemingly party around you while you struggle to buy food. You're not alone.

If there's anything I haven't addressed that you're concerned about, or if you have questions or comments, please come to my blog and share them: http://povertyprepping.blogspot.com/

You may also email me at: povertyprepping@yahoo.com

I hope the ideas I've shared with you will help you realize that you can, indeed, start prepping and build up some food storage.

Survival is going to be as much about attitude and frame of mind as it is about how we prepared. Stay positive, and try not to stress over details. There's a saying that goes "Do what you can, with what you have, where you are" (Teddy Roosevelt). It's a good one to remember.

It is only when you have done nothing that you have lost the battle. Good luck!

Other books by this author:

Non-Fiction:

Food Self-Sufficiency: Reality Check

Fiction:

A Funny Thing Happened On The Way To The Takeover (Cont. next page)

A Funny Thing Happened When We
Took Back America

The Double

A Tale of Two Preppers

The Long Ride Home

The Rally Point: Bugging Home

Over the River and Through the Woods

Back Across the Pond

Made in the USA
Lexington, KY
18 February 2013